THE HIDDEN GHOULS

NAIELA OMER

Contents

Introduction

There has always been a debate about the existence of ghosts and spirits. Spirits have always been categorized- one being evil and another good, and I have time and again heard my elders say that the good ones have never troubled anyone and they somewhat keep travelling with you to protect you from something evil and unnatural. The evil ones, well we can guess what that means and what evil is supposed to do.

One of my relative once encountered something; how should I put this in words? She was once coming back from visiting the house of a mutual dead relative, while nearing her house she felt someone following her, she heard heavy footsteps. Having enough of the man or woman following her she turned back and sternly told the person to leave her alone. Well, what did she see- nothing or no one. There was only darkness and nothing. She was terrified beyond her wits and hurried towards her house. The next day she fell seriously ill and according to her she use to hear a whisper of a male- asking her to kill herself. Thankfully, she was cured or whatever you termed it as, what must have been done to get rid of that whisper.

Now, many might believe it, many won't. I don't blame anyone. I am starting my book with a nice and catchy story. Isn't this an interesting way to introduce a book filled with supernatural beings?

I was not born in Darjeeling but grew up, studied and completed my Post-graduation in this town. While in school there were many instances and rumors of ghost being spotted in certain places. A dead pregnant lady's spirit possessing a newly married girl. A woman with open hair getting possessed by a lusty man's spirit, and many more. In school we actually had a great way of passing our time while discussing about these stories and then again reciting our own version to someone else.

My inclination towards horror came from these stories itself. I have always found this subject interesting and gripping. The chill, the silence and then the sudden burst of emotions: scream, shriek and a loud cry of fear.

I cant say if I believe in spirits or not. This is a question none wants to answer.

Someone encountering an evil spirit or something that is unnatural or not of this world or...(there are many terms to describe these elements), is scary for that particular person,(obviously) but it becomes a story for another. It becomes a narrative element for the listener and also a way of entertaining the world.

Well, we can keep discussing the varieties of scary stories and keep making different and new versions of it. There is no harm in doing that. Right?

Keeping the various ghost stories heard during her school days, the author will unfold a book for those who love to be on edge while reading or watching a horror piece.

This books is totally a fictional one. An attempt to scare the readers.

@nonilaores.

CHAPTER ONE

THE BEGINNING OF A DREAM

There was a sense of dissolve, a sense of belonging.

I had been staring at my laptop since the past one hour and yet, there was not even a single word typed on the white screen. The screen window was blank and my mind was also mirroring the same.

I stared outside, the wind was blowing at it's best tonight and the turbulence it was creating was wreaking havoc in my mind too. The night seemed eerie and the darkness outside was unnerving in a wild sense. I had never questioned my decisions or ideas, but right now I regretted coming at this god forsaken place. My original plan of seeking solace and comfort at a faraway land- with minimal population, scattered houses, and an abundant of wild dense forest was turning out to as a mistake.

The trees were tall to the extend that one would break their neck while trying to cover the whole length. The minimal population of this mysterious place consisted of very strange people, who gave away a very discomforting presence. Their eyes were like black beads with no sense of reality and naturalness in them. Staring intensely at those beady eyes, one could mistake them to be hollow sockets of the dead. They could take away your breath, drag your soul away from your body and suck on your blood- while the red liquid would drip out of those hollow sockets.

A loud clank jolted me out of my thoughts. I stood from my chair, with my single thermal blanket wrapped tightly around my body, and leaned out of the wooden window.

Nothing, except darkness was welcoming me. My eyes adjusted to the dark outside and finally, I saw an aluminium roof sheet lying on the ground. The wind was howling and my face was cold with just the little amount of leaning out. I quickly leaned back and hurriedly closed the window, but the howling didn't stop. Somewhere something was crying desperately for help. A cry of anguish and pain mixed with the howl of the wind was travelling and it seemed to be knocking on my window. I pressed both my hands on my ears and tried blocking the hideous sounds.

Although my soul was that of a kind and helpful one- I had no intention of leaving the confines of my room. There was no way, I would go outside and enquire about the howl, wind, or whatever!

I shifted my laptop, my pen and my leather diary on the bed and got settled on the cocoon of the thick warm blanket.

Taking a deep breath, I turned my attention back to the blank screen of my laptop. *I have to come up with something, there is no way I can leave this place without a perfect story with me.* My mind was filled with worry and need for a perfect story. My passion and career were at stake, and right now it felt like my life was also at stake. *Career? Do I have one.* My brain fumed at this sudden stupid thought. *Of course, I have one!*

My conscious self was at war with my true senses. *Was there something about me, that I was not ready to accept?*

The howling of the wind was not at peace at all and the cry seemed to be encouraging by each passing moment. I glanced at the closed wooden window and for a second contemplated to open it and see what was outside but my rational mind kept me frozen on the bed.

I withdrew my eyes from the window and looked around the room. A not so large, but convenient enough wooden structure. With a queen sized bed, two wooden stools on each side of the bed. A wooden almirah in front of the bed. A wooden table and chair near the now closed window. These were the basic things in the room I was residing in, and it was more that enough for me.

The room was filled with a golden glow from the old golden light bulb. I always loved this colour for bulbs rather than the boring white long tube light. But, right now the bulb was flickering, obviously due to the wind and maybe upcoming rain. It actually would be much better if it rained. Rain has always been my quantum of solace and my muse too. My mood brightened up with the idea of rain, maybe I could write something if it rains. I silently prayed for rain to pour down, not bothering it might take away the only light illuminating the room.

A creak was heard from upstairs. The cook was maybe preparing something for dinner. The house or cottage in which I had taken solace for a whole two weeks was a three storied house. The ground floor had three huge rooms more like huge halls, the only servant cleaning the patio floor, when I came three days ago told me it was this way since he had joined as a servant and he had absolutely no idea about who owned this house or the desolated land surrounding it. I kept questioning myself and my strange decision to come at this place, this god forsaken place- with no name, no proper amount of population and only some hollow eyed beings who would eat me alive by crawling up my window if I left it open at night. The thought itself made me want to puke.

I had only managed to see the three hall rooms by glancing from the main entrance when the servant rushed me to the first floor where he showed me my room which was the only room open, somewhat clean. The other rooms were locked and it seemed that they were never used, ever.

The first floor had five rooms in total and thankfully the room I was given was at the beginning of the long and dark hallway. There was no proper light in the hallway and the stairs leading downstairs and upstairs to the second floor were completely dark. I had glanced at the hallway but nothing except darkness was evident. There was a feeling of someone watching you from the dark and might just jump out of it. While I looked up and down, the servant was staring at me with a lone look. He gave me the biggest chill. His presence itself was cold and discomforting. He was standing way to close to my liking. I hurriedly created some distance between us and his eyes mocked me with his vicious stare. I masked my worried expression and stared back at him with anger. He closed his eyes and smiled lightly with his eyes closed and turned around and left me alone, much to my relief. This was the first tick of my sixth sense, yet I foolishly wanted to stay at this place, only because I had no other option and place. There were several reasons for me to come and reside at this place, but the most important one was- I had no proper place for me to stay, my mind was jumbled up with many good and bad decisions of my life. *I am desiring something which will definitely cost me my life.* This thought itself made me depressed and my life seemed much more desolate than my surrounding.

I looked up and prayed the food would be ready soon. Without nothing to do in life for a while, the human body seems to get tired really fast- that was the exact thing happening with me. There was a sudden sense of hunger and I wanted nothing more than just to eat and sleep soundly. I couldn't even recall the proper time when I had slept soundly; with my mouth slightly open and soft snores presenting my carefree self and how nothing bothered me. *That was a really long time ago. That woman is long dead and this woman right now is living her life in a dilemma. An unsure feeling; which can be her destruction or can give her a bright future. Destruction- through her ideas and a bright future if those ideas garner proper attention.*

I huffed lightly and wrapped the blanket around my body, creating a barrier between me and that male servant's vicious and maliciousstare, from the hollow beady eyes of the people of this place and also from the howling wind outside.

I slumped down with my head hanging, my brain was desperately trying to make up a nice plot, but nothing; absolutely nothing.

There was a soft knock on the door, I jumped at the soft sound. Gulping down the saliva from my dry and parched throat I asked the person to come in.

The door opened with a creaking sound and in came the cook with a small girl strolling behind her.

I sighed with relief, and smiled warmly at them. The cook, not a woman rather a girl, not more than nineteen and the little girl, her sweet little daughter.

They were the only people who radiated warmth and the only people I believed were alive in this place. Maybe because she had a soft face, a warm set of brown eyes, and a friendly smile. She came inside the room, holding a dish covered with a wooden lid in one hand and a plate with rice in the other. The room was suddenly engulfed with the smell of cooked rice, it had a sweet and calming smell which rejuvenated my sour mood. The thought and stress of not being able to produce a story was thrown at the back of my mind and for the time being, I just wanted to eat and relish in the after taste.

I smiled widely at both of them, the little girl trailed behind her mother, while holding a flask in her small and pale hands. *There was a thought-since the last three days, this duo has been bringing me food three times a day, and every time I see them both, I feel happy, I really do, but there is also a sense of familiarity. It seems I have seen them before. I can't remember how, when, and why- but I just feel I do know them. Like a long lost friend.*

The mother neared the bed, creating space for the food to be kept, I dug as soon as the food was laid for me. The sweet and warm rice, the vegetable warm, spicy and just the perfect taste. I ate my food like a glutton and I was not ashamed for my action. The little girl giggled softly, and my hands froze. That giggle, that sound...it seems, I have...

I looked up from my plate and saw the duo smiling warmly at me. The atmosphere which was replaced by them entering the room was suddenly back, it felt suffocating. I was confused. I never felt this way. *My breath seems to be taken away, my lungs feel constricted. What is happening to me?*

The rice suddenly smelled like something old, like someone old. A smell so familiar. I just couldn't pinpoint. I keep staring at their face, they kept smiling.

Both of them were standing at the foot of the bed, the mother, now with just a blank look gestured me to finish the food. The warmness of her face and smile was replaced by a cold look, the shivers returned back, I felt like I had been thrown out in the cold weather, with the howling wind and some unseen force. Something evil. Something ominous.

I shook my head and gobbled the food quickly. I was desperate for them to leave. The mother left the room with the dirty dishes, leaving the daughter behind. The little girl was standing there with a smile on her lips. *What felt warm now felt senile.*

I was on the verge of a panic attack and if the girl didn't leave at this instant, I would scream at the top of my lungs. I yet had to wash my hand, but there was no want in me-to move.

The mother appeared again, with a steel bowl and a mug of water. I was somewhat glad at this. I quickly washed my hand with the extremely cold water. My whole soul shivered with cold. The mother now smiled with her teeth showing, she looked like a witch, a complete witch. I leaned back nearing the other end of the bed. Thankfully, the duo left and shut the door behind them, not before scaring me till death- the little girl looked back and grinned just like her mother did. She stared at me for a good whole minute and then left.

I sighed deeply. This was just not normal. Since the last three days, I had never felt this way- especially not with these mother-daughter duo. The servant was a prick, a man filled with vile thoughts, there was no doubt in it, but these two were my warmth in this cold, they were my escape route. Now, they seem the most heinous among the hollow population.

I leaned back against the wooden head board and my mind drifted back to a certain memory. Something vague, something old, nostalgic- with a black and white picture. *Something that had happened some years ago? Or months ago? Or maybe days? was the picture really black, or white or there was a recent event which had stirred up this reality that I was living in?*

The wind seemed to have stopped, the cloud were now active- it was going to rain. Good! And just like that, rain started pouring down with full force.

There was an automatic force, a sudden flicker in my mind. My eyes landed on my laptop- the blank screen was desperately waiting to be filled and I was ready to fill it with many numerous words.

THE DREAM CONTINUES

There was a nostalgic feeling; a feeling of love, of care, of warmth and of sadness.

My eyes opened with a start. I looked around my surroundings, there was coldness all around. The light blub was no longer illuminating the room, the rain had stopped but there was still water dripping from the various roofs and trees. The sound was rather soothing- *everything about rain is soothing for me.* I yawned loudly and wrapped the thick blanket tightly around my small frame.

My laptop, pen and leather diary was lying on the table near the wooden window. My mind seemed to wake up properly at this. I sat up with a whip. I had no memory of leaving my bed last night. These three objects were clearly near me last night. These were supposed to be on the bed in the morning too, but there were not. Who moved these? Did someone enter my room last night. Did I not lock my room last night. Suddenly last night's events seemed to be blurry. My mind played hazy videos; remembering became a task for me now.

I shook my head, left the warmth of the bed and decided to encounter the other weird creatures of the cottage.

Finding the bathroom was as difficult as understanding this place, the first day. I had absolutely refused to venture towards the side of the second floor and the other four rooms, and continuously prayed that the bathroom would be on the ground floor. Thankfully, there was a room left to mine which gave me the hint of it being the toilet- with the strong stench of urine. I had somehow managed to finish my business and yet again use it for two days. *I was amazed at my will power.*

Today it was locked, no matter how much I tried pushing or pulling it, the nonsensical door refused to budge, my bladder was kicking me and I desperately needed to use the toilet.

I slowly walked down the stairs and came in view of the vile creature of the servant cleaning the patio, just like he was on the day I arrived here, the young mother standing near the main door of the cottage and her daughter playing with one of the rocking chairs. I remembered the cottage being almost empty on the day I arrived here, but today it seemed there were many object occupying the empty rooms. I slowly glided towards the servant, I had no intention of talking to him, but my needs were desperate too. I cleared my throat and all three looked at me. Their eyes were hollow, empty and dead, but they quickly brighten up and smiled warmly at me.

What might look warm was nothing but senile for me. I wanted to get far away from them.

My eyes moved from the servant to the mother and landed on the daughter. *Don't they have names.*

I opened my mouth but nothing coherent words came out. I was frustrated at my weakness and fear. I was being bare and open in front of these strangers and I was sure they could see my fear, sense my discomfort, read my thoughts and smell my anxiety.

I shook my head, and quickly showed them my toothbrush and toothpaste. The mother made a sound of surprise and quickly came to me. She grabbed my arm and guided me towards a room. It was at the far corner of the main hall. Her hands were as cold as ice. My entire soul shivered with cold and fear. I glanced slightly at her- she was what one would term as a perfect definition of beautiful. *She was definitely pretty, but she being alive was a question to definitely ask.*

She pushed open the door and thankfully it was the bathroom. I nodded my head at her and moved towards the loo, but the grip on my arm refused me to move. I looked down at my arm and then back at her. There it was again- the same feeling of dread and anguish. The warm smile was replaced my the grin- the grin of evil.

I wanted to cry with frustration and anger. I snatched my arm away from her, she seemed to wake up from a spell. She was back to that warm self of hers. I rushed to the bathroom slamming the wooden door loudly and locking it carefully.

The bathroom was thankfully bright enough and well kept too. It would not be a nice sight to come to an old century toilet. The room was big enough, there were two shower heads, two wash basins, two Indian style toilets at the left corner of the room and even a bathtub on the right side. Everything was in pairs out here. It seemed hilarious but not a muscle of mine stretched for a smile.

I walked towards one of the wash basin and glanced at the mirror, it was cold but I had managed to sweat. Sweat beads were scattered on my forehead and even trailed down from the side of my left temple.

I quickly finished my business and almost froze to death due to the cold water. Taking a shower was not even an option right now. If I could just ask for some warm water...

No more encounters with these vile humans.

The thought of home came up in my mind, but my heart made a sour beat to that thought. Nothing was left for me at that place. Yet, I also couldn't reside at this place a day longer.

"I have to leave..."I whispered to myself.

I closed my eyes and ran my hand on my cold face, the very next moment my eyes flew open- a raspy whispered sound filled with pain reached my ears- *"they wouldn't let you go..."*.

I kept staring at the mirror, the bathroom was empty but my lungs constricted with immense pain, my breath was coming out in short pants and I felt my face heat up again, almost till the point of burning.

"they wouldn't let you go, mind me, they just wouldn't".

This time it was not a whisper, but a proper statement, a statement which came out from a crisp voice. I jumped slightly and a soft scream came out of my mouth.

The singular whisper now took turn of many voices whispering something incoherently.

I was paralysed with fear, my mind was pushing me to run, run far away from this godforsaken place, but not a muscle moved.

A soft creak was heard, but nothing opened. The many whispers were no longer whispers and I could hear number of voice- it seemed people were talking, they were having a heated conversation. My breath were coming out in pants and my anxiety was reaching at its apex. Finally a scream broke the barrier of fear and anxiety and I bolted out the door.

I banged the door of my room and breathed heavily. My whole self was shivering with fear, the cold which had engulfed me a while ago was replaced by a scorching heat of fear and terror. *What happened earlier?*

My mind was reeling with numerous thoughts, I was shivering violently and tears graced my face.

I wiped my face, my panic stricken body slumped down on the wooden floor and I sobbed loudly.

I have to leave...I have to leave...I have to leave...

"they wouldn't let you...they wouldn't let you...they wouldn't let you..."

My ears burned with these whispering.

I wanted to die.

I have to leave...

"they wouldn't let you".

THE GROWTH OF THE SAME DREAM

THE GROWTH OF THE SAME DREAM.

Sadness was dissolved and happiness took over.

The feeling of someone watching you without your permission is the most unsettling feeling ever.

Although, I was alone in my assigned room-there was a prickly feeling of someone watching me. Who was it? I had lost all my energy to sense the identity of that unnatural person or force.

I was swiftly packing my belongings. I was not going to waste a single moment anymore.

My life was at stake and if I manage to stay here a day longer- my life would be snatched away from me.

Life is short. My life has been a tumultuous one and if I come out of this nightmare right now life will definitely give me a story worth writing.

Finally, standing at the door I glanced back at the room. Quietness and calm- contrary to what was brewing inside my mind.

I carefully walked down the wooden stairs, not wanting to encounter any one of the trio.

The sky was laden with only heavy pouring clouds, the day as gloomy and unsettling as the place and it's inhabitants.

The hall was not occupied with any one the three and there was also no presence of light. I stood quietly at the last step of the staircase and looked at the large room. Silence-yet, the feeling of dread was looming over me. The quietness of the surrounding was slicing my inner self and my body shivered from the numbing cold wind.

There was a contemplating thought in my mind- *whether to leave quietly without paying, or to look for any one of them.* I couldn't bring myself to go in search of any one, so after giving my thought another thought of a minute, I left the designated cash on one tall wooden stool.

I pulled my jacket tightly around my torso and swiftly glided down the stairs, the hill and now I was standing in the middle of the forest with no idea of a way out. Lost and scared.

CHAPTER THREE

A SUDDEN FEELING OF REALITY

"happiness was short-lived- a dark entity loomed ahead of me".

The forest was dense, deep, dark and dangerous. I had no idea what the situation was. I was trapped by my own self and now the way out of this trap was just a bleak reality.

Why did I even come here?

My life was revolving around a perfect story, a perfect plot and a gripping scenario, but my desire was taking over my reality- my life and my mind too.

Does everyone have to pay a price for dreaming a life. Why is it necessary for a person to work hard to achieve even a point in his life?

The trees were as tall as one could lift up their head or even taller than that. My whole body shivered with fear, cold, heat and languish.

My hands moved with unknown power and it seems I had no control over them.

I stood frozen on my spot with no heed of what to do next or what will happen next.

The thought of never getting out of here gave me a chilling feeling.

Finally, having enough of my helplessness, I managed to move in some direction. My head was blocked with thoughts of unknown and my heart was hammering with ferocity and my body shivered and kept shivering.

The distant sound of crickets and other insects were able to help me calm my uneasiness- a to a meagre extend. I decided to head back to the direction of the cottage, but even that seemed difficult right now.

I had completely lost the idea of it being day or night. The dense forest was like a thick blanket which isolated me from the outer world. The forest was filled with numerous sounds- which were difficult to comprehend.

Taking a deep breath, I walked towards a long hollow path. It seemed I came from that direction but, anyways.

Not thinking twice, I grabbed my luggage and swiftly started covering the path.

My steps were faltering due to the various sounds coming from all directions. I had managed to keep up with my path and not stop.

I had managed to reach halfway when I spotted light. My whole body filled with relief.

I quickened my pace and as I neared the light I saw a small wooden house. A single wooden house. The light was coming from that house and it seemed there was nothing else rather than this house.

Finally, I managed to cross the whole hollow path and come out of the forest- Alive.

I was shocked to see, it was already night and a night which might me darker than any before. A single light was enough for the revival of my hope but not enough for me to walk in this opaque darkness. I shuffled in my jackets pocket, and a chill ran down my spine. My cell-phone was not with me.

I suddenly had no memory of checking whether I kept my phone with me or not. The desperation to leave from that cottage had cost me my entire life.

I had my whole self in my mobile and now it was gone, lost or where I don't know.

I screamed desperately with frustration and anger at myself. *I am a total waste of this earth*

Tears streamed down my dry face and in a minute I was sobbing loudly. Slumping down on the muddy ground, I buried my face in my hands.

Suddenly, there was someone or something beside me. I jolted violently when I felt a hand on my shoulder. My body ran out of blood when I saw a man, tall, leaning down at me with an evil grin and sockets empty of any eyes in them. I cried loudly when his grin grew wider. I managed to push myself far away from him but I was numb with fear.

He stayed rooted on his place, but leaned down more towards me.

I cried some more and he laughed at my misery. The sound of his laugh echoed in the entire surrounding. I shifted backwards, stood up and leaving all my belongings sprinted towards the house.

The door was open, I landed on the floor and cried for help to whoever was in the house.

My skin prickled with fear, I looked back and saw the same man standing at the door, with his hands behind him- with the same grin, empty sockets and his face seemed to be clear now.

I covered my eyes when I saw blood coming out of his hollow sockets. He laughed again.

There was putrid smell of flesh decaying and my whole self got drenched with a hot sense of fear and alarm.

I looked towards the source of the smell, forgetting the man in front of me. My heart skipped a bit when I saw a group of people hunched towards a body of human being- the body was dripping blood and was being eaten alive by these group of people.

I screamed loudly, frozen at my spot.

All movement stopped and everyone turned to face me. My eyes grew wider when I saw, the servant, the mother and the little girl- desperately licking the blood of their hands. They looked the same as the man- wide evil grin, hollow sockets and blood dripping from their mouth and eyes.

The little girl giggled and the rest of the group returned back to satiate their hunger. The body, dead or alive looked at me with eyes bloodshot and tears running down his face. I shuffled back swiftly till my back hit a something or someone.

I heard the laugh again and a pair of hands landed firmly on my tired shoulders. Howls were heard everywhere. There seemed to be more of them.

The grip on my shoulder was out of my strength and there was nothing that could help me right now.

I desperately thrashed for the hands to let go me but they wouldn't budge. I got a glimpse of the person holding me- the same man, mouth open widely, with blooded teeth and hollow bloody eyes.

I screamed again.

THE REALITY UNFOLDS

"death loomed above me, no one to save my soul"

My hands were above my head and my eyes drenched with tears. I was begging this creatures to let me go, but they simply laughed at misery.

My flesh was hurting everywhere and my bones seemed to crack- as the man dragged me back to the forest- deep inside the arena of death.

I thrashed my legs but now everything seems futile. I was tired and my body was losing out the little amount of energy it possessed.

I sobbed silently.

The howls kept on increasing and the creatures walking alongside kept murmuring amongst themselves. Some laughed while glancing at me, some licked their lips and some were still chewing the body parts of that now dead person.

I am going to be eaten alive by these unnatural things.

My death looked down at me and smiled sickly at me.

I closed my eyes, now ready to accept whatever is going to come forth, when suddenly everything stopped.

I opened my teary orbs to come face to face with the little girl. The man was still holding my hands and little girl leaned down to my face. I cried helplessly and she smiled with a victorious smile. I shielded back from the putrid smell radiating from her. She smelled rotten, dead and without any life. The warmth I had once felt coming from her aura was replaced by something I didn't want to feel or smell.

"please..."

I had managed to speak.

She stood up, now with a blank expression.

"You bought this on yourself, you shouldn't have left us..."

I furrowed my brows at her blank statement. I was confused beyond measures. *What did she mean?*

She kept murmuring the same statement again and again and gradually the whole crowd chanted the statement.

"you bought this on yourself, you shouldn't have left us..."

My ears burned with these words and I wanted them to stopped.

I screamed for them to stop, but they developed a certain stance. The man left my aching hands and joined the others. The howling creatures now circled around me and kept chanting the words.

They went on and on and on...

"stop, please stop..."

I begged them to do so. They kept completing their trance.

The little girl was the only one who stood away from them, she neared me, I jumped back a bit. She grabbed my left foot and shockingly dragged me back. I wailed and wailed- but no one was showing mercy.

The evil child now sat on top of me and her little hands strangled me. The force she was applying was unbearable and I was losing my self.

I pushed her face, but she kept squeezing life out of my body.

Death is an inevitable thing. Something that can't be avoided. I see death right in front of my eyes. Death was nearing me. I was dying...I am dying. My body is floating through the unseen passage of time. My soul seems to be diverted my flesh. I am dying...

I jolted upward with a violent start. My whole body was sweating profusely.

Suddenly, I took notice of my surroundings. I was no longer in that god forsaken place, but in the safety of my house. In my bedroom. Sitting upright on my bed, with my parents and sister surrounding me- a worried expression on their faces and sudden realisation of all that being a horrible dream of mine.

My sister offered me a glass of water, which I gulped down thankfully.

"What happened to you?" my younger sister asked.

I gestured for her to wait.

With my voice still hoarse I told her it was a horrible nightmare.

She sighed softly followed by my parents.

I smiled sheepishly at them.

My father kissed my forehead, petting my hair softly. My mother hugged me warmly and they left my room.

My elder sister smacked my forehead lightly and left with a laugh.

"sleep some more". She called behind her.

I left out a short breath and slumped down on my soft breath.

Nightmare...

Everything felt so real. So much like my reality and so much filled with pain.

The glanced out of my window, bright rays of winter sun streamed on my face. I smiled softly.

Just a dream.

I whispered to myself.

ONE YEAR LATER

JUST A DREAM?

"happiness of living your dream".

I smiled at my laptop screen.

The email was finally send, and my very first book was on the verge of being published.

This was happiness for me.

While I cried for a perfect plot, there was already one- which was left incomplete by me, written during my school days.

I dreamed a plot, a story and even managed to live it in my mind.

The little girl, the mother, the servant, those hollow creatures- all characters of my story.

The words they chanted brought sense in me and I somehow managed to find this story thrown carelessly in our store-room.

I laugh at myself.

What a way to remember something forgotten?

Shutting down my laptop, I walked towards my window.

The wind was cold. Another winter had arrived. I loved this season.

The shop were now almost closing for the day, everyone was preparing to go home. Glancing around the busy *mohalla,* that we live in my eyes landed on someone.

My whole body shivered with pain and fear, my hands twitched in their own and sweattrickled down my forehead when I spotted the little hollow eyed girl. Standing across my house- with a grin she lifted her hands and summoned me towards her self.

I let out a soundless scream and my body collapsed down on the floor.

Something wet fell on my face, I opened my eyes.

My whole world turned upside down, when found myself in the same cottage room, on the bed with the howling creatures looming over me- with blood and laughter, ready to devour me.

I screamed again.

©nonilaores.

Author's Note.

This book has been yet another one of challenge for me to complete, yet I loved writing every hit of it.

I just hope the readers will love reading it as much as I loved writing it.

Thanks to all those YouTube horror stories I went through.
Naiela Omer.
©nonilaores.